## Turbulent Planet

# Crumbling Earth

## Erosion & Landslides

Mary Colson

Raintree

**www.raintreepublishers.co.uk**
Visit our website to find out more information about Raintree books.

To order:
☎ Phone 44 (0) 1865 888113
▤ Send a fax to 44 (0) 1865 314091
▭ Visit the Raintree Bookshop at **www.raintreepublishers.co.uk** to browse our catalogue and order online.

First published in Great Britain by Raintree Publishers, Halley Court, Jordan Hill, Oxford OX2 8EJ, part of Harcourt Education Ltd.
Raintree is a registered trademark of Harcourt Education Ltd.

Editorial: Charlotte Guillain and Isabel Thomas
Design: Michelle Lisseter and Bridge Creative Services Ltd
Picture Research: Maria Joannou and Virginia Stroud-Lewis
Production: Jonathan Smith
Printed and bound in China and Hong Kong by South China Printing Company

Originated by Dot Gradations
ISBN 1 844 43112 6
08 07 06 05 04
10 9 8 7 6 5 4 3 2 1

**British Library Cataloguing in Publication Data**

Colson, Mary
Crumbling Earth : erosion – (Turbulent planet)
1. Erosion – Juvenile literature 2. Natural disasters – Juvenile literature
551.3'02

A full catalogue record for this book is available from the British Library.

**Photo acknowledgements**

p.4/5, PA Photos/EPA; p.4, Popperfoto; p.5 bottom, FLPA/D Fleetham, Silvestris; p.5 middle, PA Photos/EPA; p.5 top, Oxford Scientific Films/T. C. Middleton; p.6, FLPA/Silvestris Fotoservice; p.6/7, Getty Images Imagebank; p.7, Oxford Scientific Films/Roland Mayr; p.9, NASA; p.10/11, Oxford Scientific Films/John Downer; p.10, Rex Features; p.11, FLPA/USDA; p.12/13, Corbis/Lloyd Cluff; p.12, Corbis; p.13, Corbis/Bettmann; p.14/15, PA Photos/EPA; p.14, Oxford Scientific Films/David Tipling; p.15, Oxford Scientific Films/Alastair Shay; p.16/17, Corbis; p.16, FLPA/Mark Newman; p.17, Corbis; p.18/19, Corbis/Jonathan Blair; p.18, OSF/Kynan Bazley; p.19, Science Photo Library/NASA; p.20/21, Corbis/Ron Watts; p.20, PA Photos/Martin Keene; p.21, Alamy/Worldwide Picture Library; p.22, PA Photos/Chris Ison; p.23, Associated Press; p.24/25, Skyscan; p.24, Corbis/Elio Ciol; p.25, Corbis/James L. Amos; p.26/27, Magnum Photos; p.26, Oxford Scientific Films/T. C. Middleton; p.27, Corbis/Kim Kulish, Saba; p.28/29, Corbis; p.29 right, NASA Goddard Laboratory for Atmospheres/Hasler, Peirce, Palaniappan, Manyin; p.30/31, Corbis/Annie Griffiths Belt; p.30, Associated Press; p.32/33, Corbis/Bob Gomel; p.33, Corbis/David Butow; p.34/35, Oxford Scientific Films/Richard Packwood; p.34, Oxford Scientific Films/Keren Su; p.35, Oxford Scientific Films/Andrew Park, SAL; p.36/37, Corbis; p.36, FLPA/Wendy Dennis; p.37, Rex Features; p.38/39, Corbis/Galen Rowell; p.38, Oxford Scientific Films/Stan Osolinski; p.39, FLPA/D Fleetham, Silvestris; p.40/41, FLPA/E. & D. Hosking; p.40, Naturepl/Martha Holmes; p.42 left, Ecoscene/Tony Page; p.42 right, Ecoscene/Andy Rockall; p.43, Associated Press; p.45, Corbis/Lloyd Cluff

Cover photograph reproduced with permission of Corbis

Every effort has been made to contact copyright holders of any material reproduced in this book. Any omissions will be rectified in subsequent printings if notice is given to the publishers.

**Disclaimer**

# Contents

Any words appearing in the text in bold, **like this**, are explained in the glossary. You can also look out for them in the Wild words box at the bottom of each page.

# Our crumbling Earth

△ A mudslide
covers a car.

## Sudden change

All of a sudden, the ground under your feet starts to
shake. As you struggle to stay standing, the whole world
starts to swing and sway. You cannot keep your balance.
Everything is starting to fall down.

You look up to see the hillside starting to move. Slow at
first, the loose earth quickly becomes an **avalanche** of
mud and rocks. It streams down the hill towards your
town. As it falls, it gathers speed and grows in size. It
knocks down trees and gathers more earth and huge
rocks. The ground has stopped shaking but the land has
started sliding. Nothing can stop it. As earth races
downhill, huge rocks **tumble** and crush animals, crops
and buildings.

avalanche   mass of snow, ice, rocks or mud falling fast down a mountain
erosion   wearing away of the Earth's surface

## Panic

The landslide rushes down, crushing houses and burying cars. It is getting faster and bigger all the time. Roads are blocked and transport is at a standstill. People are screaming and trying to outrun the moving earth. They try to gather a few **precious** belongings before it is too late. Some escape with nothing but their lives.

Panic sets in as everyone rushes to find their loved ones. Names are shouted. People help each other to dig and search. There is no time to waste. With the rain starting to fall, another landslide could happen at any moment.

## Find out later...

*Is all **erosion** harmful?*

*How many landslides happen each year around the world?*

*What different types of people study erosion?*

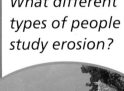

precious   valuable, important
tumble   fall, especially quickly and violently

# World in motion

The surface of the Earth is changing all the time. Most of the changes are so small you cannot see them. Some changes are very noticeable. **Avalanches**, fires and landslides are some of the most dramatic examples of sudden change.

## Creeping earth

The surface of the Earth can change in many different ways. High winds swirl around mountains and through **valleys**, knocking off bits of rock and picking up soil and dust. Sand carried by the wind wears away at rocks, creating fantastic shapes. Rain batters down on fields and rivers, washing away land. **Glaciers**, or ice rivers, carve mountains into amazing shapes and create valleys. Finally, there is the difference that over six billion human beings make to the way the Earth looks every single day.

△ Liquid rock bursts out of volcanoes and hardens, building up domes of new land.

glacier   slow-moving river of ice
process   series of steps

This **process** of change is called **erosion** and it is happening all the time. Some erosion is natural. Some of it is caused by humans. Some erosion is good and some is very bad. Erosion is what happens when the surface of rock or soil is worn away by wind, water, air, fire and humans on the planet. Erosion affects us all.

## Natural cycle

Many of the changes are normal processes that create some of the planet's most amazing natural wonders. Millions of tourists visit the Grand Canyon every year to marvel at the rock patterns, colours and amazing scenery. This is one example of how the Earth's surface has changed shape over millions of years – and it is still changing today.

### Changing Earth

- The Grand Canyon has been shaped over nearly a billion years.

- Each year there are tens of thousands of landslides and **avalanches**. Luckily, most take place high up in mountains and far away from people.

More than 5 million people visit the Grand Canyon every year. ▽

△ Strong waves batter and shape the rocks along the coastline.

**valley**   low area of land between hills or mountains

This cross-section of the Earth shows the different parts. ▽

In order to understand some of the natural **erosion** or land change that is happening, we need to take a look at how the Earth is made up.

## Three-part planet

Our planet is made up of three main parts. In the very middle is the **core**, a mass of ultra-hot rock. Scientists can only **estimate** how hot the core is but it is thought to be around 5500 °C, as hot as the Sun's surface. The outer core is liquid and the inner core is solid rock. Next to the core is the **mantle**, where boiling gases and liquid rock bubble away. On top of the mantle comes the Earth's **crust**. This is an outer layer of rock. All the sea and land that we know sit on top of it.

## Jagged jigsaw

Unfortunately, the Earth's surface or crust is not in one piece. It is broken up into about thirty main pieces or plates. Some of these plates are enormous. For example, the whole of Africa sits on one and the whole of North America is on another.

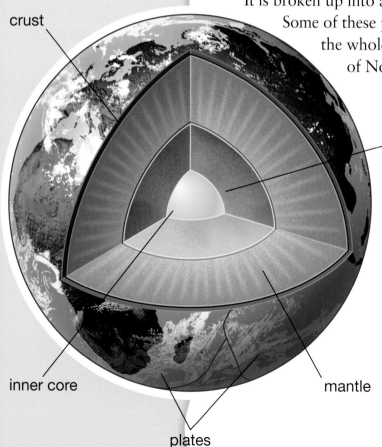

crust

outer core

inner core

mantle

plates

**Key to the Earth's plate margins**

—— **Constructive margin** Two plates move away from each other

▲▲ **Destructive margin** Oceanic crust moves towards continental crust and sinks beneath the continental rock

—— **Collision zone** Plates made of continental crust move towards each other and crumple upwards to form fold mountains

▲▼▲ **Conservative margin** Two plates move past each other

continent   land mass
erode   slowly wear away

Heat escaping from the Earth's core causes these massive plates to move and press against each other. This movement creates mountains, **valleys**, seas and earthquakes. It can even make volcanoes erupt. The plates move against each other at different speeds and in different directions. This movement of the plates is called **plate tectonics**. Plate tectonics creates and destroys landscapes.

The ground that we stand on is changing all the time. The shapes of the **continents** are changing very slowly as waves **erode** the coasts and earthquakes crumble the land.

The Atlantic Ocean ▷ is getting wider. The Eurasian plate is moving away from the American plate by about 5 centimetres every year.

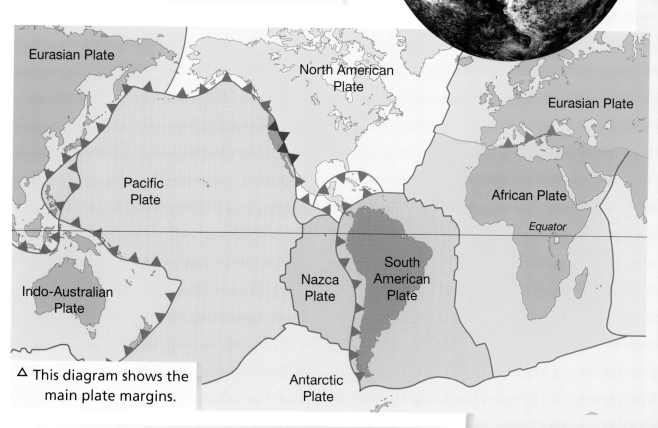

△ This diagram shows the main plate margins.

Eurasian Plate

North American Plate

Eurasian Plate

Pacific Plate

African Plate

*Equator*

Indo-Australian Plate

Nazca Plate

South American Plate

Antarctic Plate

mantle    super-hot gases and liquid rock that surround the Earth's core
plate tectonics    movement of the Earth's plates

## Earthquake in India, 2001

After a powerful earthquake, the town of Bhuj lay in heaps of twisted concrete. Buildings were torn in two. Over 90 per cent of Bhuj was not safe to live in.

## Plates at war

There is bound to be a disaster when two massive lumps of rock press against each other or pull apart. Earthquakes happen when two plates grind past each other and stick. The pressure between the two plates builds up so much that one plate has to give way. As it gives way, the ground moves.

When **shockwaves** from an earthquake reach the surface, the top of the Earth's **crust** crumbles. Buildings **tumble** and roads crack. On 26 January 2001, an earthquake struck the town of Bhuj in India. Bhuj was directly above the **focus** or starting point of the earthquake. This point on the surface is called the **epicentre**.

△ There was no electricity, no running water and no shelter in most of Bhuj after the earthquake.

eruption   when a volcano explodes
focus    source of an earthquake deep underground

## Chain reaction

Sometimes when plates move deep underground, they set off a chain of events on the surface of the planet. This is called a chain reaction. One way these underground movements are seen on the surface is when a volcano erupts. This can cause a lot of damage and **erosion** of the Earth's surface.

Deep underground, super-hot liquid rock and gas are under great pressure. Slowly, this **magma** melts the rock above it and moves upwards. It pushes through holes in the Earth's crust called **vents** and makes new plate or crust. As the magma rises up, it causes movement in the Earth's crust and can start earthquakes.

### Volcanic explosion

One of the largest **eruptions** of the 20th century was caused by an earthquake. On 18 May 1980, Mount St Helens in the USA was shaken by an earthquake. The volcano erupted violently. An **avalanche** of rock and mud moved at 240 kilometres (150 miles) per hour.

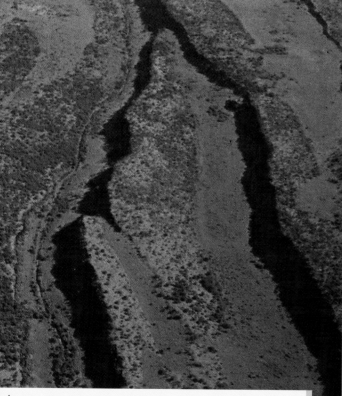

△ The Montanas del Fuego (Fire Mountains) in Lanzarote are a group of **extinct** volcanoes that formed at the north-west margin of the African plate.

△ Over 500 square kilometres (200 square miles) of forest was destroyed by the Mount St Helens eruption.

**magma**   super-hot liquid rock and gas underground
**shockwaves**   forces that are created by an earthquake deep underground

# Fragile planet

**Did you know...?**
After the earthquake in 1906, San Francisco burned for three days. The fire did more damage than the original quake.

The Earth is more **fragile** than it looks. Here are some ways natural forces shape the surface of our planet.

## San Francisco shake

An earthquake is a shaking of the Earth's **crust**. Very often, the real **erosion** happens after the ground has stopped shaking. In 1906, an earthquake shook San Francisco, USA. It took just 48 seconds of shaky ground to cause millions of dollars of damage. Land cracked and split and roads were **buckled**. The shaking broke gas pipes and the city was quickly in flames. Fire raged through the wooden buildings.

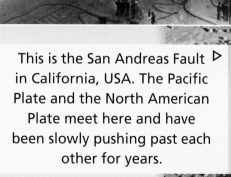

This is the San Andreas Fault ▷ in California, USA. The Pacific Plate and the North American Plate meet here and have been slowly pushing past each other for years.

buckle    twist or bend out of shape
fragile    delicate

The 1906 quake was the first time an earthquake hit a region that had been studied carefully. Scientists measured everything before and after the earthquake. They learned a lot about how the plates of the Earth's crust move against each other. They studied how earthquakes **erode** the surface of the planet.

## Terrifying tsunamis

Earthquakes can start landslides, cause flooding, make volcanoes **erupt** and spark fires. They can also set off big ripples of energy across the surface of the oceans.

These ripples cause huge waves, or **tsunamis**. The waves can be up to 30 metres high, but are usually between 3 and 15 metres. Tsunamis travel across the ocean at an average speed of 750 kilometres (470 miles) per hour. The waves grow even taller as they reach the coastline. The huge rush of water damages rock and washes away soil.

### Fragile facts

- The longest recorded earthquake was in Alaska in 1964. It lasted four minutes.

- The tallest recorded tsunami hit the coast of Alaska in 1958. It was 518 metres high!

- The 2001 Gujarat earthquake in India killed at least 20,000 people.

△ Around 30 blocks of flats were damaged or destroyed in Anchorage, Alaska by the 1964 earthquake.

**tsunami**   huge ocean wave caused by earthquake, landslide or volcanic eruption

Some rocks are softer than others and they erode or break up quickly. Limestone is a very tough rock but it can still be eroded. Rivers, sea, wind and acid rainwater can all change limestone.

## High-level danger

People who live high above sea level in hills or mountains may be safe from floods. But they face danger from another dramatic way that the Earth is **eroded**. Landslides **occur** all over the world and for all sorts of reasons. A landslide happens when rocks and earth slip and **tumble** down hillsides. Landslides cause **erosion** as they change the face and shape of hillsides. Earthquakes, heavy rains and human mistakes can all cause landslides.

## Quake wrecks El Salvador

In January 2001, a powerful earthquake struck parts of Central America including the small country of El Salvador. Thousands of buildings were destroyed. Roads were blocked and power was cut off. Many people were killed when the quake caused a landslide. Hundreds of houses were buried as thick mud slid down a mountain.

Over 500,000 people were left homeless by this landslide in Honduras, South America in 1998. The slide was **triggered** by heavy rain. ▷

△ This rock formation in Ireland is known as the Limestone Pavement.

occur    happen
severe    very bad or serious

## Volcano slides on to village

In November 2001, a landslide from a volcano buried a village in Nicaragua. Matters were made worse by **severe** flooding in the area. Helicopters tried to reach the village but over 50 people were killed before help arrived. The mudslide was caused by heavy rainfall. The slopes of the volcano simply slid down, forming a mud river. This got faster and faster and gathered more and more earth as it fell. The village did not stand a chance.

### Caving in

The largest cave in the world is in Malaysia. The Gunung Mulu National Park has a cave that is 700 metres long and 70 metres high.

△ Rock erosion can have many good effects. Caves provide homes for hundreds of **species** of plant and animal.

**species** type of plant or animal
**trigger** cause something

This multicoloured rock formation in Western Australia is known as The Wave. It is 15 metres high and was shaped by erosion. ▽

Sometimes rocks move quickly and sometimes they move slowly. But over time, the results can be dramatic. As rocks move, they **erode** other rocks and soil and can create new natural wonders in their place.

## Uluru

Some of the oldest rocks on the Earth are also the most famous. Uluru or 'Ayer's Rock' in Australia is one of the most recognizable rocks in the world. It was formed over 500 million years ago. Sand piled up on the bottom of an ocean that once covered the middle of Australia. As a result, this huge sandstone rock was created. Over the years, wind and rain have beaten at the rock and eroded the surface of it.

The land around Uluru was once the same height as the rock. Millions of years of erosion left only the rock standing. ▽

### Fragile facts

- The base of Uluru (Ayer's Rock) is 8 kilometres (5 miles) around.

- Uluru is over 300 metres high.

- Uluru is thought to be the tip of a mountain that extends many kilometres below the desert floor.

rift   breaking apart, separation

## The Victoria Falls

One of the greatest waterfalls in the world lies where the Zambezi River drops into a deep **gorge** between Zambia and Zimbabwe in Africa. It is an amazing sight to see water spray rising over 300 metres in the air. The falling water makes a mighty roar as it plunges down. But the falls would not be there if the rock had not moved. The falls were formed by a deep **rift** in the rock that lies directly across the path of the Zambezi River. The rift was caused by movement of the Earth's **crust** about 150 million years ago. The rift meant that the rock slid down, making the river fall with it.

Locals call the Victoria Falls 'the smoke that thunders'. ▽

# Trial by water

## Expanding ice

When water freezes, it turns to ice. As water freezes, it grows bigger by about ten per cent. This means that a 100 millilitres of water will freeze to give 110 millilitres of ice. This is how water cracks, breaks and erodes rock.

Changes happening deep underground also affect the surface of the planet. But the causes of **erosion** can be found above ground too. Water has been shaping land for millions of years.

## Slow silent stream

About 24,000 years ago, much of the Earth was covered in ice. This was called the **Ice Age**. The land was frozen. The ice was thick and very solid. But it was not still.

Slowly, over time, the **expanded** ice cut into the rock and carved **valleys** and mountains. It created some of the scenery and coastline we still see today. The coast of Norway is very rugged with lots of small bays. These bays were carved by **glaciers**. Glaciers are ice rivers, left over from the Ice Age. They are slow and silent and they gradually erode rock.

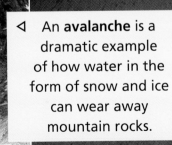

◁ An **avalanche** is a dramatic example of how water in the form of snow and ice can wear away mountain rocks.

expanded    made bigger
Ice Age    time when ice covered much of the world

## Bird's-eye view

**Marine biologists** study life underwater. Marine biologist Geoff Carlier went to South America to study glacier movement. He described what he saw in his diary as he flew over some glaciers in Patagonia, southern Chile.

Glaciers can be huge. They can fill your whole field of vision with white. From the air, they look like big white motorways. At the end of the glaciers are ice cliffs and <u>icebergs</u>. These are a very rich blue colour. Glacier Grey is one of the biggest and it is getting bigger all the time. The ice river flows down to a glacial lake where there are lots of icebergs. You can watch huge chunks of ice as big as hotels just fall off the end into the ocean.

### Fragile facts

- The fastest glacier in the world is in Alaska, USA. The Columbia Glacier can move up to 35 metres per day.

- The world's largest glacier is the Lambert Glacier in Antarctica. It is at least twice the size of France.

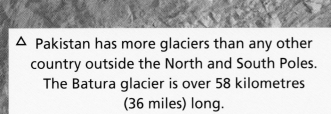

△ Pakistan has more glaciers than any other country outside the North and South Poles. The Batura glacier is over 58 kilometres (36 miles) long.

△ The Lambert Glacier is being studied by scientists. They want to see if it can help them **predict** climate changes on the Earth.

**iceberg**   chunk of ice that falls off a glacier into the sea
**marine biologist**   scientist who studies life in the sea

## The mark of time

In the Northern Territory of Australia, Katherine Gorge has been created by a river passing through the rock over millions of years. The steep sides of the **gorge** mark the passage of the river where it has eroded the rock.

## Carving canyons

Rivers flow to the sea, leaving their dramatic mark on the landscape. The Colorado River in America is a winding stretch of water, hundreds of miles long. Over time, it has **eroded** deserts and mountains to make a passage through the land. It has even carved out the Grand **Canyon**.

The sun bakes the soil of the Grand Canyon until it is bone dry and hard. It does not rain often, but when it does the ground is too hard to **absorb** the rain. The rain pours down into the Grand Canyon, taking large rocks with it. Some of these rocks are bigger than cars. In the winter, water gets into cracks in the rocks and freezes, causing more **erosion**.

△ Katherine Gorge in Australia was created by erosion.

absorb   soak up
canyon   deep gorge

# River ruin

Rivers all over the world erode land. Millions of people live along the world's largest rivers and depend on them for food. Rivers can be dangerous and erode structures like buildings and bridges. When they flood they can destroy farmland and erode the soil.

About 400 million people live near the Yangtze River in China. Along the river, there are forests, many different breeds of wildlife and millions of kilometres of farmland. The waters of the Yangtze are used for rice **paddies** and to water wheat fields. When the river floods like it did in 1997, hundreds of thousands of people faced starvation because the rice and wheat crops were washed away and the land was ruined.

## Water, water

The Amazon basin holds one-fifth of all the flowing water in the world. Over 1000 rivers feed into it. If we cut down the forests, we will lose water and land. Many animal and plant **species** would be lost for ever.

The Grand Canyon follows the path of the Colorado River for over 445 kilometres (265 miles).

△ The Amazon river is the largest river in the world in terms of its volume. It runs through six South American countries including Brazil, Peru and Ecuador.

gorge    narrow valley between hills or mountains
paddy    waterlogged field for growing rice

## Water, water everywhere...

Over 70 per cent of the Earth's surface is covered by water. Water has been slowly shaping the land for millions of years. It can change the landscape slowly over time or in just a matter of hours. Floods, rain and waves all **erode** our world. **Erosion** can have serious effects on people's lives.

## Disaster: Flood!

Floods are the worst kind of natural disaster because they cause the most damage. Farmland is made useless as crops are **waterlogged** and the **topsoil** is washed away. This makes it harder to plant new crops. Floods also wash away minerals in the soil that help crops to grow. Homes are destroyed and drinking water is quickly made dirty. Leaking **sewage** can **rapidly** spread disease. In poorer countries, people may have a long wait before help arrives.

### River disaster

When the water level gets too high, rivers burst their banks and flood. In 1887, 900,000 people were killed when the Yellow River in China burst its banks. Thousands more died from starvation and disease after the floods damaged crops.

Land near a wide river is ▽ at risk of flooding.

rapidly    with great speed
sewage    human toilet waste

# Flood focus: Mozambique, 2000

The floods of 2000 were the worst to hit Mozambique in Africa for more than 150 years. A series of tropical storms caused three weeks of **severe** floods. At times, the wind reached 260 kilometres (160 miles) per hour. Over half a million people were forced to leave their homes. Roads, bridges and farm crops were all destroyed. People who had lost everything stayed in camps, where disease spread quickly. Food was donated from other countries.

> " From the air, the amount of water is stunning. The tops of trees and thatched huts and ruined crops are the only things you can see. "
>
> An aid worker describing what she saw in Mozambique.

### Flood figures

- The cost of flood damage in the USA is more than US$3 billion a year.

- An average of 10,000 people have died each year since 1900 because of floods.

This helicopter is rescuing flood victims from a roof top in Chibuti, northern Mozambique. ▽

topsoil    best layer of soil for growing plants
waterlogged    soaked with water

## Ebbing away?

Some of the greatest **erosion** on the planet is caused by the sea. The sea has the power to change coastlines, washing away rock as waves crash against it. Waves can make cliffs collapse and beaches shrink.

*The South Coast Times*  
*12th January 1999*

## Cliff crumbles!

A huge chunk of the cliff at Beachy Head on the south coast of England crashed into the sea yesterday in a massive landslide. The cliff was weakened by heavy rain and on 11 January, it crumbled. Thousands of tonnes of rock fell away from the cliff face. Scientists say large waves hitting the cliffs are to blame. Each time a wave hits, it sends **vibrations** up the cliff and makes the rock weaker.

The spectacular cliffs at Étretat in France were shaped over time by waves
▽ eroding the rock.

△ There is little left of Hallsands village today after a storm in 1917 washed most of it away.

breakwater   barrier built in the sea to protect a coast or harbour from waves

Sometimes the results of wave erosion are spectacular, like at Étretat, France, or the Isle of Wight in the UK, where the waves have shaped magnificent limestone arches and pillars. Other times, the results are disastrous.

## Time and tide

Over a century ago, many tonnes of **shingle** were removed from the beach of Hallsands village on the south coast of England. The shingle was used to build a **breakwater** in the city of Plymouth.

In the years that followed, storms continued to attack the south coast. Now that the village had lost its natural defence, erosion happened quickly. With nothing to defend it against the lashing waves and howling winds, the village was swept away. Many people lost their homes and jobs.

△ More than 1 million cubic metres of sand have now been deposited along the 5 kilometre (3 mile) shoreline of Danfuskie Island in South Carolina, USA.

**shingle** pebbles
**vibrations** small shakes or tremors

# Blowing up a storm

The weather plays a part in changing the Earth. Too much rain, sun or wind can do a lot of damage to the landscape. **Weathering** is when rocks are broken down or worn away by the effects of weather. Changes in the weather can make weathering happen.

## Taking a beating

**Geologists** study rock and how it moves and changes. They also study **erosion** and work closely with weather scientists called **meteorologists**. Between them, these scientists study how erosion and weather change the surface of the planet.

Wind, rain and sun all erode the surface of Earth. Wind picks up sand and small bits of earth and blows them away. Rain washes away **nutrients** from soil and makes it less **fertile**. Too much sunshine can kill plants, ruin crops and make the ground too dry to grow things in.

△ The Arches National Park in the USA is full of incredible rock formations caused by erosion.

evaporate    turn into water vapour
fertile    able to grow things

## A dry spell

A drought happens when rainfall drops below a certain level. Where there is sunshine all the time, not many plants can grow. The sun makes water **evaporate**. This means that ponds, streams and rivers dry up. The sun dries out the land so that it is no longer able to grow plants. Even if it does rain, the ground is too dry to soak up the water and the top layer of soil is worn away. This means the land is useless for growing food.

## 'The child'

In 2002, some countries were badly affected by freak weather. Something called *El Niño* is to blame. *El Niño* is a warming of water temperatures in the Pacific Ocean. This affects the weather around the world.

*El Niño* means 'the child' because it happens around Christmas time each year.

### Widespread effects

In 2002, *El Niño* caused:

- droughts and flooding in America, Australia, India and Europe.

- heavy rain in Italy, resulting in mudslides in towns and cities

- a record numbers of forest fires.

△ The country of Ethiopia in north-east Africa often suffers from severe drought. The average Ethiopian lives for just 43 years compared to an average of 78 years for the UK and Australia.

△ The landslide that wrecked these houses in California, USA was caused by *El Niño*.

**meteorologist**   scientist who studies weather
**nutrient**   substance that helps things grow

# Storms

Powerful winds that spin through the air are called **cyclones**. The strongest and most destructive of these winds are **hurricanes** and **tornadoes**. They also have the power to create **storm surges**. This is when the wind makes the sea rise up into giant waves that crash against the shore. These winds have the power to change the landscape in seconds.

# Nightmare in paradise

In late 2002, the powerful Cyclone Zoe swept across the **remote** Solomon Islands in the Pacific Ocean. The cyclone reached speeds of over 200 kilometres (125 miles) per hour. A TV cameraman who flew over the islands said, 'All I saw were forests stripped bare. I could not see any homes left standing. It was total devastation.'

Buildings are no match for a ▷ hurricane. With its terrific speed and strength a hurricane will destroy everything in its path.

cyclone    tropical storm
hurricane    storm with strong, violent winds

# Savage storms

Bangladesh is a tropical country in Asia. It is large and low-lying. This means that it has a lot of land that is only just above sea level. Bangladesh often suffers from floods. The cyclone that struck the country in 1970 was the worst tropical disaster of the 20th century. Over 300,000 people died as winds of over 200 kilometres (125 miles) per hour struck the country.

The hurricane that hit Galveston in Texas, USA was one of the deadliest natural disasters in American history. Before the hurricane, Galveston was an ordinary town. That changed on 8 September 1900. The wind swirled around at over 225 kilometres (140 miles) per hour. There was a storm surge of 5 metres. It cost over US$20 million to repair and rebuild the town.

## Counting the cost

The most expensive storm in history was Hurricane Andrew, which struck southern Florida in late August 1992. It caused widespread damage to industry and farming. Thousands of square kilometres of crops were destroyed and the estimated cost was over US$26 billion.

△ Hurricane Andrew was recorded travelling at speeds of 285 kilometres (170 miles) per hour.

**storm surge**   high waves caused by strong winds
**tornado**   funnel of fast, spinning wind

## Wear and tear

As the wind blows, it picks up little bits of sand and earth. When this sandy wind moves across the landscape, it blows these particles against hillsides and the ground. The sandy wind wears away at mountains like sandpaper. Bits of rock are knocked off and the rock is worn away.

Crops are quickly blown down by winds like this. Because the wind also damages the soil it is also harder to plant new crops. The central part of the USA has wide flat fields where lots of wheat is grown. This wheat is used for making bread and the whole area is called America's '**bread basket**'. When these winds whip across the land, they destroy the wheat.

**Path of destruction**

Every year in the USA farmers face the threat of **tornadoes** ruining their crops. It only takes a few seconds for a tornado to destroy a harvest.

△ This spinach field was completely wiped out by **Hurricane** Floyd in 1999.

bread basket    area important for growing crops
sand dune    sand hill

## Sand mountain

A **sand dune** is a mound of sand that has been left by the wind. Dunes are found in sandy areas like coastlines and deserts. They are lots of different shapes. Some are long and thin and others are like stars. It depends how the wind blows the sand into shape.

Sand dunes do not stand still. They move with the wind. If the wind is very strong, they can be carried several kilometres at a time. Sand dunes have ruined growing crops, blocked roads and even buried houses. When the wind picks up the sand from a dune, it can **erode** rock even faster.

### Sand sea

- Death Valley, USA, has a **sand sea**. Nothing grows there because the temperature is over 50 °C.

- The world's highest sand dunes are in Algeria, Africa. At 465 metres high, they are taller than the Empire State Building in the USA.

△ The world's longest sand dunes are found along the Skeleton Coast of Namibia.

**sand sea**   large area of moving sand

# The human effect

## Welsh tragedy

In 1966 in Aberfan, Wales, 144 people were killed when a **slag heap** moved after heavy rain. It slid on to a school and many children and their teachers were killed.

Humans **erode** the planet 24 hours a day, 7 days a week. Lots of things we do, from using cars to throwing away rubbish, change the Earth in different ways.

## Food for thought

We need the Earth to grow food and provide energy. Oil is pumped out of the ground to fuel our cars. Chemicals are extracted from the oil to make everything from building materials to medicines. We need our planet to work well, but sometimes it all goes horribly wrong.

Prince of Wales Sound, Alaska, 1991

## Oil on water

Over 1.4 kilometres (0.9 miles) of coastline remain ruined by a massive oil spill two years ago. Forests, parks and wildlife are all suffering and thousands of birds have been poisoned. The previously beautiful coast was turned into an **oil slick** in 1989, when the *Exxon Valdez* tanker spilt enough oil to fill 125 Olympic swimming pools. Scientists fear this may be the most **environmentally** damaging oil disaster in history.

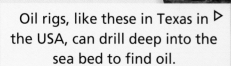

Oil rigs, like these in Texas in ▷ the USA, can drill deep into the sea bed to find oil.

oil slick   layer of oil floating on the sea
pollute    make air, water or land dirty or impure

# Mining minerals

Coal, oil and gold are just some of the things that we dig out of the ground. This is called mining. Most of the time, mining is safe, but when too much is taken out of the Earth, it can lead to disaster.

In 1903, a small coal-mining town in Canada learned a tragic lesson. Over seventy people were killed in Frank when a landslide on Turtle Mountain devastated the town. The landslide was caused by coal-mining inside the mountain and **weathering** of the limestone on the outside of the mountain. Once the rock started to slide, there was no stopping it. 82 million tonnes of rock fell in 90 seconds. Entire houses were swallowed up.

**Did you know...?**
Cars **pollute** the air badly. When petrol burns, it releases poisonous gases like carbon monoxide.

△ The air in a traffic jam is polluted by poisonous gases.

slag heap    pile of waste rock from a mining site

## Timber!

All over the world forests are being cut down at an alarming rate. Areas of forest are often cleared for farming. **Deforestation** is man-made destruction. The worst deforestation happens in tropical areas, like rainforests. These forests produce a lot of the oxygen we need to breathe.

Forests are also destroyed by **pollution** from factories. Pollution is when poison and waste enter the **environment**. The factories and cars that burn **fossil fuels** like coal or gas are the worst. The smoke they produce contains poisonous chemicals and gases. When these mix with water in the air, the result can be awful. Instead of normal rain falling so the trees in the forests can grow, something much more harmful falls out of the sky instead.

**rain water + poisonous chemicals = acid rain**

### Safe steps

In some tropical countries where landslides are common because of heavy rainfall, farmers terrace their fields. They shape hillsides into steps so that crops can grow there. The plant roots help to bind the hillside together and prevent landslides.

△ Rice terraces like these are common in China and Southeast Asia.

fossil fuel   coal, oil or natural gas
habitat   home

## Acid attack

The smoke and chemicals dissolve in the rain water and make it more acidic than normal rain. Each year, thousands of square kilometres of forest are affected by acid rain. It eats away at leaves and roots and eventually kills forests. When the trees have gone, the soil is soon **eroded**. Crops may not grow in these areas and there is more danger of landslides because there are no roots to hold the earth in place.

## Forest facts

- Forests cover only 25 per cent of the planet's surface.
- In 2002, National Park managers in the USA started to let **logging** and mining companies work in parks.
- 71 per cent of forests in the Czech Republic are affected by acid rain.

## A price to pay

We need wood for all sorts of things from making paper to building houses. But logging can erode natural **habitats** for animals, **pollute** rivers and break up the forest soil structure.

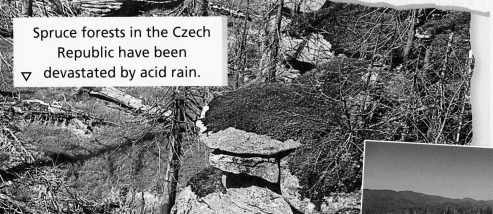

Spruce forests in the Czech Republic have been ▽ devastated by acid rain.

△ Many forests today are sustainable. This means that new trees are planted to replace those that have been cut down.

**logging**    cutting down trees and selling the wood
**deforestation**    when forest is removed, burned or destroyed

# Polluted air

Making sure there is enough food for everyone is a huge industry around the world. Farmland is very important in all countries. In lots of places, forest or grassland is cleared so that crops can be planted. This can have disastrous effects. The forests are often burned to clear them quickly and cheaply. The smoke is very dangerous to humans. It can cause **asthma** and other breathing problems.

In 2001, there were lots of fires in Indonesia as farmers tried to clear forest. The **smog** from the fires affected 50 million people in six countries. Over 40,000 people went to hospital because they could not breathe properly.

△ During drought the land dries up and is easily eroded.

asthma    lung disorder that makes breathing hard
drought   severe lack of rainfall over time

# Dustbowl

In the 1900s, the central and southern US states were mostly natural grassland. There were thousands of square kilometres of 'spare' grassland and the government wanted the land cleared to grow wheat. The wheat would then be used to make bread.

The grass was removed and wheat was planted. By 1930, all the soil had become dry and loose as a result of the change from grass to wheat. This part of the USA is very flat and windy. The wheat did not hold the soil together and protect it from the high winds as well as the grass had. **Drought** followed and the soil was easily **eroded** when strong winds whipped through the region. The dust created by the soil clouds gave the area the name of Dustbowl.

## Fragile facts

- The type of grass that was cleared away in the USA before the 1930s is now planted to stop **sand dunes** moving. It is called esparto.

- The Aral Sea in Asia is shrinking. Much of its water was taken away for farming programmes and the sea has started to dry up.

Giant duststorms in America's dry mid-west have been known to ▽ block out the sun for several days.

△ The Aral Sea was once the fourth largest inland sea in the world. Now it is drying up.

**famine**    serious shortage of food
**smog**    fog or haze caused by smoke or pollution

## Off the beaten track?

Everyone loves to go on holiday. But when lots of people want to do the same thing, it can cause problems for the **environment**. The movement of all these people on the Earth's surface **erodes** the rock and soil over time.

Kate and Ben Smee travelled from their home in London to see Yosemite National Park in the USA. They were hoping to find some peace and quiet in the natural **wilderness**. They were **dismayed** to find themselves in the middle of an enormous traffic jam. 'It was incredible,' Kate said. 'End to end cars throughout the park.'

Sarah Morris was very excited as she packed her rucksack to go on safari in Tanzania. But it was not exactly the wild Africa she had been hoping for. 'There were 30 large jeeps full of tourists parked around a tiny hippo pool. It was like being in a traffic jam.'

### Spoiled beauty

Lots of people travelling means more **pollution**. There will be fumes from cars, buses and aeroplanes and there will be extra litter. This will affect the beautiful places people have visited to enjoy.

△ So many tourists visit Yellowstone National Park in the USA that traffic jams often happen.

dismayed    disappointed
ecosystem    relationship between animals and their environment

# A great barrier

Imagine a chain of millions and millions of multi-coloured animals and plants floating in a clear blue sea. Each tiny piece of that living chain is an important part of one of the biggest, most important and **fragile ecosystems** on Earth: the Great Barrier Reef.

The Great Barrier Reef lies off the coast of Australia. It is thousands of miles long. Every year thousands of visitors come to dive and snorkel. Amelia Brock went diving in this natural wonder. 'It was absolutely amazing. All the fish and coral were so brightly coloured and there were so many of them! But you could see damaged and dead coral where diving equipment had been dropped on to the reef. There were also lots of boats **moored** near the reef with their engine fumes and oil spilling out.'

## Reef facts

- In 2003, the Australian government decided to ban fishing and shipping in almost a third of the Great Barrier Reef.

- The reef is **monitored** by marine biologists every day. They test the water for pollution levels. The reef is a World Heritage Site.

Crowds flock to photograph animals in the Ngorungora Conservation Area in Tanzania. They could be destroying the **habitat** of the very animals they come to see.
▽

△ The Great Barrier Reef attracts thousands of divers every year.

moored   when a boat is tied up
monitor   check

# Erosion in the future

## Ice caps

- The North and South Poles are massive areas of ice.

- They are home to many plants and creatures, such as penguins and polar bears.

- If the Earth gets hotter, the ice will melt and sea levels will rise, causing flooding.

The **greenhouse effect** is actually a natural **process** that controls the balance of heat inside the Earth's **atmosphere**. The gases in our atmosphere trap some of the Sun's heat as it is reflected back to space. This makes the Earth around 30 °C hotter than it would be otherwise. So natural greenhouse gases are important for all living things. But when humans release carbon dioxide and water vapour into the atmosphere these gases add to the natural greenhouse effect, heating up the planet more than usual. This is known as **global warming**. Scientists have predicted that the temperature everywhere on the Earth will rise by 3 °C over the next 100 years.

Global warming could melt huge areas of the planet's ice caps, causing flooding ▽ around the world.

△ The **habitats** of Arctic and Antarctic animals are under threat.

atmosphere   layer of gases surrounding the Earth and other planets
**global warming**   rise in the Earth's temperature over time

## Hole in the ozone layer

A layer of ozone gas surrounds the Earth and filters out some of the harmful ultraviolet (UV) light rays from the Sun, which cause sunburn and skin cancer. Gases called chlorofluorocarbons (CFCs), used in refrigeration, air-conditioning, cleaning solvents, packing materials and aerosol sprays, damage the **ozone layer** and make it thinner. UV rays can pass through gaps in the ozone layer, damaging living things. The thinning of the ozone layer also adds to global warming. The use of CFCs in aerosols has now been banned in many countries. But other chemicals, such as nitrogen oxides from fertilizers, may also attack the ozone layer.

## The forecast

Global warming may cause dramatic changes to the weather. Summers might become extremely hot and cause deserts and **droughts**. Winters might be **severely** cold. Sea levels will rise as the polar caps melt, causing flooding in low-lying countries. Spring rains might not stop until rivers have burst their banks, ruining farmland. Nobody can be sure quite what global warming will bring, but the changes in the weather may speed up the **erosion** of the planet's surface.

### Warming planet

- Global temperatures have risen 0.6 °C over the last 100 years.

- The UK is warmer now than at any time in the past 200 years.

- Scientists think that because of global warming, parts of south-east England and the USA could be under water by 2050.

---

greenhouse effect   trapping of heat by gases like water vapour, carbon dioxide, methane and nitrogen oxides

## A cycle of renewal

**Erosion** does not always destroy the planet. Sometimes nature recycles materials over thousands of years. The rock cycle is like this. Mountains are worn away and the small pieces that are **eroded** become soil. Soil is blown or washed away to become **compressed** as new rock on the ocean floor. In other places, volcanic **eruptions** will create new mountains. So the land does renew itself, but it takes a very, very long time.

## Making a difference

Lots of groups and organizations work hard to make the Earth safer and cleaner. Greenpeace and Friends of the Earth are two international organizations who talk to governments and people about environmental **issues**. Being 'green' means you are helping the planet by recycling things or trying to stop **pollution**.

△ Groynes are built out from beaches to trap sand and shingle.

Many teams of **volunteers** ▷ work to repair the effects of erosion in their spare time.

**compress**　squeeze together
**issue**　important subject for discussion

Erosion can be controlled through sensible farming and **logging**, and by being more careful with our waste products. For many people, it is a choice about they way they live. We can all make a very quick difference if we do not produce so much rubbish ourselves. Things like cans and bottles can be recycled so they do not clog up rubbish dumps. Could all that fast-food wrapping and packaging be avoided?

## The future

Every single day, the Earth crumbles a little bit more. Some of this erosion is natural. Some of it is not. Land, water, wind and humans all play their part in the changing face of our planet. Some things can be used again. Some things do not have a second chance. Think about it.

After all, there is only one Earth.

### Health risk

Mexico City is the most polluted major city on Earth. The air is so bad, there is a **permanent** haze or **smog** over the city. Millions of people who live there have breathing problems.

Some residents of Mexico City wear masks to protect themselves from harmful smog. ▽

permanent    always there
volunteer    person who is working for free

43

# Find out more

## Organizations

### The Earth in our Hands

An excellent website by the British Geological Society, answering all your questions about the causes and effects of landslides.

geolsoc.org.uk/pdfs/
Landsldes.pdf

### US Geological Survey

The national site for landslide information in the USA, including news on the most recent slides.

landslides.usgs.gov

### BBC Science

News, features and activities on all aspects of science and natural disasters.

bbc.co.uk/science

## Books

*Awesome Forces of Nature: Crushing Avalanches*,
   L. and R. Spilsbury (Heinemann Library, 2003)
*Discovering Geography: Weather*,
   Rebecca Hunter (Raintree, 2003)
*Landscapes and People: Earth's Changing Mountains*,
   Neil Morris (Raintree, 2003)
*Nature on the Rampage: Landslides*,
   Jim and Ronda Redmond (Raintree, 2003)

## World Wide Web

If you want to find out more about landslides and erosion, you can search the Internet using keywords like these:

- lanslide + news + [date you are interested in]
- 'acid rain' + landslide
- deforestation + erosion
- effects + 'global warming'
- plate tectonics + KS3

You can also find your own keywords by using headings or words from this book. Use the search tips on page 45 to help you find the most useful websites.

## Search tips

There are billions of pages on the Internet, so it can be difficult to find exactly what you are looking for. For example, if you just type in 'water' on a search engine like Google, you will get a list of 19 million web pages. These search skills will help you find useful websites more quickly:

- Know exactly what you want to find out about first
- Use simple keywords instead of whole sentences
- Use two to six keywords in a search, putting the most important words first
- Be precise – only use names of people, places or things
- If you want to find words that go together, put quote marks around them, for example 'sand dune' or 'acid rain'
- Use the advanced section of your search engine
- Use the + sign to add certain words, for example typing + KS3 into the search box will help you find web pages at the right level.

## Where to search

### Search engine

A search engine looks through the entire web and lists all the sites that match the words in the search box. They can give thousands of links, but the best matches are at the top of the list, on the first page. Try **bbc.co.uk/search**

### Search directory

A search directory is more like a library of websites that have been sorted by a person instead of a computer. You can search by keyword or subject and browse through the different sites in the same way you would look through books on a library shelf. A good example is **yahooligans.com**

# Glossary

**absorb** soak up

**asthma** lung disorder that makes breathing hard

**atmosphere** layer of gases surrounding the Earth and other planets

**avalanche** mass of snow, ice, rocks or mud falling fast down a mountain

**bread basket** area important for growing food crops

**breakwater** barrier built in the sea to protect a coast or harbour from waves

**buckle** twist or bend out of shape

**canyon** deep gorge

**compress** squeeze together

**continent** land mass

**core** ultra-hot centre of the Earth

**crust** Earth's outer layer of rock

**cyclone** tropical storm

**deforestation** when forest is removed, burned or destroyed

**dismayed** disappointed

**drought** severe lack of rainfall over time

**ecosystem** relationship between animals and their environment

**environment** the world around us

**epicentre** point at which an earthquake reaches the Earth's surface

**erode** slowly wear away

**erosion** wearing away of the Earth's surface

**eruption** when a volcano explodes

**estimate** make an educated guess

**evaporate** turn into water vapour

**expanded** made bigger

**extinct** exists no more, dead

**fertile** able to grow things

**focus** source of an earthquake deep underground

**fossil fuel** coal, oil or natural gas

**fragile** delicate

**geologist** scientist who studies rocks

**glacier** slow-moving river of ice

**global warming** rise in the Earth's temperature over time

**gorge** narrow valley between hills or mountains

**greenhouse effect** trapping of heat by gases like water vapour, carbon dioxide, methane and nitrogen oxides

**habitat** home

**hurricane** storm with strong, violent winds

**Ice Age** time when ice covered much of the world

**iceberg** chunk of ice that falls off a glacier into the sea

**issue** important subject for discussion

**logging** cutting down trees and selling the wood

**magma** super-hot liquid rock and gas underground

**mantle** hot gases and metals that surround the Earth's core

**marine biologist** scientist who studies life in the sea

**meteorologist** scientist who studies weather

**monitor** check

**moored** when a boat is tied up

**nutrient** substance that helps things grow

**occur** happen

**oil slick** layer of oil floating on the sea

**ozone layer** layer of gas in the upper atmosphere that protects the Earth from the Sun's harmful UV rays

**paddy** waterlogged field for growing rice

**permanent** always there

**plate tectonics** movement of the Earth's plates

**pollute** make air, water or land dirty

**pollution** harmful things in air, water or on land

**precious** valuable, important

**predict** informed guess that something will happen in the future

**process** series of steps

**rapidly** with great speed

**remote** a long way away

**rift** breaking apart, separation

**sand dune** sand hill

**sand sea** large area of moving sand

**severe** very bad or serious

**sewage** human toilet waste

**shingle** pebbles

**shockwaves** forces that are created by an earthquake deep underground

**slag heap** pile of waste rock from a mining site

**smog** fog or haze caused by smoke or pollution

**species** types of plant or animal

**storm surge** high waves caused by strong winds

**topsoil** best layer of soil for growing plants

**tornado** funnel of fast, spinning wind

**torrential** strong, fast-moving

**trigger** cause something

**tsunami** huge ocean wave caused by an earthquake, landslide or volcanic eruption

**tumble** fall, especially quickly and violently

**valley** low area of land between hills or mountains

**vent** hole in the Earth's crust

**vibrations** small shakes or tremors

**volunteer** person who is working for free

**waterlogged** soaked with water

**weathering** breakdown of rocks by exposure to weather

**wilderness** natural area

# Index

# Raintree freestyle Curriculum version

## Series in the *Freestyle Curriculum Strand* include:

Turbulent Planet

Energy Essentials

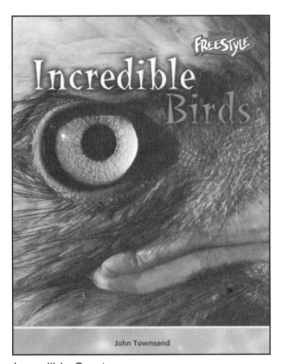

Incredible Creatures

Material Matters

Find out about the other titles in these series on our website www.raintreepublishers.co.uk